The Different Path

Poems by
Pat Underwood

BLUE LIGHT PRESS
1st WORLD
PUBLISHING

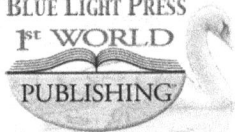

The Different Path

BLUE LIGHT PRESS
www.bluelightpress.com
Email: bluelightpress@aol.com

1ST WORLD LIBRARY
PO Box 2211
Fairfield, Iowa 52556
www.1stworldpublishing.com

Cover Art: *March Drift* by Gary Bowling
Book Design: Erik Ievins, Blue Light Press
Author Photo: Sailor Breez Photo & Film

FIRST EDITION

ISBN: 978-1-4218-3594-5

Library of Congress Cataloging-in-Publication Data

Acknowledgments

With deep appreciation, I wish to thank the editors of the following magazines and anthologies in which my poems first appeared:

Blood and Thunder; Musings on the Art of Medicine: "French Toast," "Two More Days"

Borders Poetry, The Des Moines National Poetry Festival: "Bouquets of Jellied Gasoline"

Coe College Department of Music, Elaine Erickson, Composer: "Iowa Fields"

Des Moines Register: "In the Deep Night of Winter"

Encore Prize Poems, National Federation of State Poetry Societies: "Guernica," "The Leaves at Branson"

Illinois State Poetry Society: "Thresholds"

Lyrical Iowa: "Bird Calls at the Mall," "Roses," "The Pearl"

National League of American Pen Women: "At Calvary," "Montgomery 1955," "On Slavery," "The Loggerhead," "The Many Ways," "We Believed in Angels"

Pandemic Puzzle Poems: "Taking a Knee"

Spanning the Bridge of Time: "Iowa Fields"

The Briar Cliff Review: "His Return," "The Different Path"

The Disciple: "Listen to the Children"

The Midwest Quarterly: "Plates"

Turning the Pages of Time: "Turning"

Voices International: "Forgive Me," "The Dance Floor"

Writer's Digest: "Epitaph," "On the Steps"

Author's Note

I'm grateful to the Editorial Board of Blue Light Press for choosing *The Different Path* as a finalist in this year's full-length poetry competition. Many thanks to editor Diane Frank for her dedicated support of poets and poetry. I appreciate the fine work of book designer Erik Ievins and the book team at Blue Light Press. I'm indebted to Gary Bowling for his generous gift of the cover art, *March Drift*, to Sailor Breez Photo & Film for my photograph, and to my friends in various writing groups for their constructive criticism and nurturance. Michael Carey's and Jeanne Emmons' thoughtful insights have been invaluable. Always, thanks to my family for their constant love. Most especially, thank you to George Barlow for his encouragement and for his belief in me— my ballast, my light, my sail.

for George

KITTEN CRIES

HIGH ABOVE THE QUARRY

HIS RETURN

TIRED OF GIVING IN

INFINITY

Ink runs from the corners of my mouth.
There is no happiness like mine.
I have been eating poetry.

— Mark Strand 1934–2014

I Know the Spider Personally

There's an iridescent thread
just outside my window,

rising and falling
in the laughter of the breeze.

I watch as it catches
the wink of the morning,

shimmering in green light
like a dash of nothing in air —

a stretched tightrope
searching for a snare.

I look twice to see
the deeper purpose

of one metallic strand.
Is it transportation,

nuisance,
something's livelihood?

If I could, I would fill my life
with mystery.

I'd invite you
into my laced domain.

We could play scrabble,
then I'd eat you for lunch.

KITTEN CRIES

Searching the Haymow

The mother cat thin and gaunt,
my brother and I give her milk at the door,
rush to the barn, climb the ladder.

Hay prickly against our knees,
pigeons coo at the cupula
like marbles stuck in throats.

We listen for kitten cries
where flashlights shine
into each hole, where we bend low
in the scent of alfalfa.

Hearing small meows
we pull out one at a time,
cradle each in our arms,
hold cheeks close to softness.

The babies feel our touch,
hear our sweetened whispers.

We study colors, markings,
and name each newborn —
joy a beam of light in a cranny
deep as contentment itself.

Wind in the Pines

the family voice
I felt in my throat
— Elizabeth Bishop

We twirl in Grandfather's pines, dizzy on resin.
Amidst the buzz of bees, we can almost taste

the wind as it brushes our lips, tousles our hair,
whistles through timber like a single flute

playing "Summertime." Cardinals flame our tents
of green; my brothers chase rabbits across

a pine-needle carpet. A nested robin's egg,
some stray rain — we giggle within a spider's net,

stretch shirts to lap pinecones. Our magical
backyard haven is a world of pine trees and play,

breathless running, endless taunts, forever caught
in a web of laughter.

Map of Safety

I was six, jumping
on the great hump of our cave
like a billy goat with thundering hooves.
In the darkness milk was stored,
thinly-woven baskets of golden apples,
gunny sacks packed
with odd-shaped potatoes,
onions, carrots.

Afraid the old roof would crumble,
you had it pushed in.

All these years later, Grandfather,
a lump swells thick in my throat.
My son lies in a hospital bed,
the room cave dark,
his leg weak as a willow limb
from the accident.

I remember the deep lines of your face,
your map of safety.
I wish I could have saved him —
like you, Grandfather, saved me.

On the Steps

I'm ten, draped in innocence.
The neighbor boy and I are kissing
on Grandmother's front steps.
Soft lips brush my cheek
again and again.

The door opens.
What are you two doing?
It's Grandmother.
You're never to see each other again!
Tony's feet fall to the sidewalk
like wounded raven wings.

I walk to the kitchen.
Stomach aching,
I smell homemade rolls,
fried chicken, mashed potatoes,
creamed corn.
Silence is thick as the snows of winter.
Sex is a taboo subject.
So is kissing.

Grandmother ignores my tears,
tells me to place knives and spoons
to the right of the plates,
forks to the left,
rigid and hard.

One Last Story

My grandmother would pause
at the kitchen door —
grey hair neat in its net,
flowered dress outlining
the smallness of her frame,
the occasional click of her teeth.

Holding the screen open,
facing the yard,
she would mumble a story
about someone she knew,
perhaps John Stringer,
tracing him back to childhood,
reciting long details of his death.

All this while Mother
was in the utility room ironing,
straining to hear the low drone
of something being said.
Mother would exclaim,
Why does she do that?
I can never hear her!
I can't take it any longer!
before I thought Grandmother
was out of earshot.

Tonight,
I pause at Mother's door.
I hold it open as I'm leaving,
face the outside
as I tell her one last story.
Mother bites her tongue,
listens to the slap of wind
against the screen.
Like the occasional click of futility.

French Toast

First, the crack of shell
and spilling yolk,
then milk soaking the bread.
With bacon's quick fry
and fresh-squeezed juice,
you devour morning's meal.

It was a rough night, Mother,
you behind your walker
wandering around the house —
sunlight only in your mind.

Toilet calls, cold calls, hot calls.
Charles, can you hear me?
Is anyone here?
Are you taking me home?

This is our Sunday sleep in,
our French toast of thankfulness.
We survived another night
of lost memories. And with
God's help we will
make it through another.

Salt

level plummeting, Mother faints
while eating dinner, doesn't know
my brother when she wakes

at the hospital. Mind swirling,
she sees laughing girls in glasses
near the ceiling. She strikes a nurse

with a ninety-year-old hand,
grabs a purse, joins my brother
as he's leaving, gown swimming

open. Nurses stretch to catch
her quick body. They sedate her,
face falling into carrots back
in the room. It's dangerous now.
Five salt pills a day. Last week
she organized an Elvis party for fifty —

DJ and dinner. She was dancing.
She knows part of her is missing
as laughter melds into self,

as wit disappears. Ask a math
question, ask her to critique a story
I've written, ask how to spell

any word, but she can't remember
grandchildren's names.
I think I'm losing my mind.

I tell her how brains shrink,
how arteries harden, how salt levels
must stay even. Seven years later

she's still shining.
Still hearing our voices,
Mother quietly slips away.

Undertow

through the sweet
curdle of the fields, where the plums
dropped with their load of ripeness
— Stanley Kunitz

An audience of swifts follow
    my father where he plows,

each turn of earth
    folding back on itself

like the undertow of sea.
    He imagines seeds

in the dark Iowa loam
    are pearls woven in soil,

their hard coats softened,
    blooming above the mounds

to color the land in green stalks,
    the pure gold of corn.

Epitaph

I am six. We are in the shop,
crowding in to watch your steady hands

grip the steel-tanged hammer.
We make boats,

weight them with nails
so they balance in horse-tank puddles.

Even as an adult, Father,
I am clumsy with a hammer.

Now at your grave,
I place the fern at your headstone,

balance it so it doesn't tip
beside the horse-tank grey of granite.

The Different Path

Bones shivering, eyes unclear,
the way behind you beaten to stone,
you meet me at the forest's edge.

We build a fire, and the air warms.
We talk, and songbirds
burst open their throats.

When you leave for home
you take a different path —
where a small waterfall breaks over
the rocks, where wild blackberries
taste sweet across your tongue.

I stay to watch tadpoles swim
in a pool of slow-moving water —
gills turning to lungs, tails
growing into the legs of a frog.

Walking on, I find a flower
uttering itself to the sun,
and it's you, blossoming.

Miss October

for Scott

I took her down
five years after my husband died.

She'd been hanging in the workroom
forever — dusty hips, aging breasts.

Her shapely legs crumbled
as I seared her in the burning barrel.

How could I have known
my son's sadness

when he saw she was missing?
It was a death to him.

How could I have known
the light that spilled over his face

each time he slowed to stare at her
while he grew from child to manhood

taking in his naked hanging beauty?
I wonder if he still thinks of her

when fall comes and delight nods
through the month of October.

Parasailing at Lani Kai

for Clint and Arlene

Swept off your feet,
you rise to a perfect billow,
the boat's good steer,
the tug of a rope
unfurling like a heart string
where you level above the water.

In that rich air,
this is the flight of love.
You press your palms together,
teeth gleaming, descend.

Six years later,
this is your wedding day.
Your feet are on the ground,
firm, ready to begin married life,

but you soar bright as a parasail
lifting off from the beach at Lani Kai,
red billow above your heads,
shining bright in Florida sun.

At Dead Horse Canyon

in memory of Gary

At 59,
my brother wants to buy a mule.
He loves the way
the ears fall lengthy and lean,
loves the way
the legs are long and lanky.

He'd let it run
at Dead Horse Canyon
where the old ways
are steady and strong,
where the color of solitude
is green timber, pastures of blue,
and the bend in the Little Sioux.

In the barn,
he pretends to bay at burrows.
This life after divorce
is a new experience —
like the birth of a mule
that never gives up —
perfect stubbornness —
the crazy moment of arrival.

Love Letters

The winter air at Camp Lejeune
fills with cool salt wetness.
Aunt Chloris and Grady Jackson
dance at the hall, stroll into shimmering

nights, sing old songs. It's December 31,
1943, and the two marines fall in love.
Grady transfers overseas.
Half his lungs are blown out

at the Battle of the Bulge. His love letters
drip with honey, saturate with missing her.
He writes, *I know the difference
between lust and love.* He writes

of a future ring, a home with five kids.
Her letters slow. After meeting again,
he writes, *Do you even know
what desire is? Is this goodbye?*

These many years later, I'm in her
bedroom swooning over Grady's picture.
It's always been at my aunt's bedside —
kind eyes, wavy hair, the hint

of a smile across his face. *What
happened?* I ask. *We just drifted apart
after the war,* she tells me, nonchalant
as the fly dizzy at my head, settling

on the armchair. Sad how they parted
after years of his fiery letters. Sad
about the war, his injury. Sad, the slip
of his pen about those five kids.

At the Veteran's Home

Summer afternoons of fried chicken
and baked beans at the park,
smacking our lips over the salads,
spreading out the pies. Winter
evenings reading by the fire
with good wine and oatmeal cookies,
watching embers turn to ash.

It's been a good life, Aunt Chloris.

But here at the Veteran's Home
you ignore Ensure on your tray,
the milkshake Mother and I brought
for you, cool and delectable,
that you no longer swallow. How

glad your eyes at seeing us, how
sad this final parting. How private
are your thoughts of war, your
blood of sacrifice. When you sleep,
we leave for home. The doctor calls,
choking back her tears.

Plates

for Jon

My cousin emails a picture
of New Zealand's Emerald Lake
in the crater of an extinct volcano,
a blue puddle in a pile of snow,
and it's mesmerizing.

He's there skiing in July,
hot enough to melt his boots
when steam rises on North Island.

Calcium deposits have smoothed
to rock, sunken shells
are limestone, rotted trees
are the splendid black of coal.

Where the wrybill wades
in braided rivers, its bill
curved to the right for food
under riverbed stones,
the glowworm hauls in
its fishing line of silk,
emerging from giant snails.

The translucent frogs,
hearts seen beating,
hop among flightless kiwis
that prod prey by sense of smell,
by acute hearing.

My cousin goes home to Arizona,
the plates of earth below us
forever moving.

Bird Calls at the Mall

for Keith Ratzlaff

At Jordan Creek Mall,
it's unusual to hear birdsong
floating through the shops,

over the footsteps,
down the corridor.

This is how you find Treva —
a simple whistle
within throngs of people,

a lover who calls
with bird song,
like an oriole who knows
how magical finding
a partner can be.

Night Stars

in memory of Barbara Robinette Moss, author of
Change Me into Zeus's Daughter

Facial bones misshapen by hunger,
the child rocks herself to sleep. Her father

consumes his paycheck at the tavern —
head back, whiskey ravages his throat.

He stumbles home, slaps and berates her,
the mother's face in a passive trance.

Add the overcrowded classroom,
the underfunded school. But wait!

The teacher awards her with A's. Her dad
pays for braces. A surgeon funds reshaping

her face. At twenty, she drives to the edge
of town, follows a new road where

strangers in cities relax her shoulders,
love her paintbrush, her pen. At last,

she inhales the perfume of roses,
whispers *hello* to the bright night stars.

Two More Days

for Shawna and Jeriah

Off the bypass,
off the machines,
everyone celebrates.

Everyone's hope fills
to the brim and overflows.

But the heart must contract,
must force blood into the aorta.
She is missing a ventricle.

Baby Brenna,
skin soft as a feather,
eyes big as valentines,
breathes two more days.

HIGH ABOVE THE QUARRY

The Pearl

Here in the emergency room
the doctor shows me the stone
that's stuck in my kidney,
sculpted and brilliant as a rare

pearl. I can see its tight trap
on the CAT scan screen,
feel its five-millimeter pain
attack my back like a wedged

rock. Tomorrow the doctor
will clear away this hurt,
but today I'm a sloth unable
to climb the cecropia tree,

my voice faint when nurses hook
my arm, my chest to monitors,
when need fills the room with trust.
This will pass, time the great

mender, but for now
I'm caught in this hospital bed
like my seawater pearl
struggling to be free.

Ultrasound

This morning my heart pulses
as if it could be twice itself.

I lie on a hospital table,
gel covering my chest.

I view the ominous look inside,
drink in the ebb and flow

of chambers wild with valves
that flap like teakettle lids

lifting from the steam.
The technician stills the computer,

marks the photo of my wrong beats.
With so much more of God to know

this muscle is a vessel
that fills to overflowing.

Foraging

Slowly, we heal after the fire.
Stumbling over weakened floors,
smoke and grit at nostrils,
our hearts are a sea of sorrow —

our elkhound didn't make it.
We forage what's left: grandmother's
vase, dishes, damaged photos.
Buying land up the hill, we drill

through shale, find a river
that sustains a well. We build,
brightening like orioles weaving
a nest, intricate and deep, orange

brilliance catching the sun.
In the blue autumn these years later,
tonight's sunset is a fierce fire
where it rages the western horizon.

Our home is an open window
to the sprawling oak beside us,
to the shagbark hickory, magical
in their yearly shower of nuts,

a bountiful haven for foraging squirrels.
We remember our beloved pet —
silver tail curled over her back,
eyes, full of love, melting us.

On Listening

Curled at the foot of my bed,
dawn filling the quiet room,
Yoshi lifts his mastiff head.

It's 7:45 a.m. I begin to stir.
A cough, a morning moan,
a rustle of sheets. He listens.

Yoshi, is that you?

Wiggling, twisting to my
bedside, tail thumping
the bedframe, he strokes

a wet tongue across my palm
like a paint brush splashing
bare wood. My blanket

falls back upon the bed.
My feet touch the floor. I lean
down, embrace his beautiful

jowl, scratch his colossal
chest, wide as a leopard's. He
follows me to the door,

feet waltzing for breakfast
and play only steps away.

The Invasion

It's enough to make you dizzy
when you step outside the door —

how a million moths swim the air,
how they attack and attach

with gentle legs that cling
to your hair and wrists,

the sidewalk and grass. They line
the door glass and deck rail

asking to slip inside. And they're
lovely, dressed in browns

and whites, spreading wings
like small butterflies. Wind

doesn't phase them. The dog doesn't
deter them. They flutter and fly,

open and shut versatile hinges,
multiplying in this June heat

like pesky little nuisances
borne to make you love them.

Osprey

They nest high above the quarry,
adjusting to feed their young,

flying intermittently for fish.
We are the watchmen,

tilting our necks to see
lovebirds at the edge of town,

rare to see, hear, and almost
forgotten. The father hovers,

adjusts the angle of his flight
against refraction, against

a fish's distortion. Nostrils
closed, he plunges his body

into the water. Talons
rounded, reversible, he grasps

the slippery prey. The white
head, dark mask, rises

into summer air — a fish hawk
who teaches a town to feel

the beating of his tiny,
intricate, amazing heart.

Burning the Ditch

In the smallest shelter from wind
match and flame befriend, ignite
brome and foxtail like a broom
sweeping the steepness of the bank.

Enough multi-floral rose remains
to brace earth from erosion —
this yearly ritual by the dusty road
where I listen to the voice

of the linden, its resting place
for the wren, where just up the hill
tribes waved deerskin over fire
and smoke puffed over bluffs.

My neighborhood was a town —
miners and a railroad, Barney Oswalt
and his fiddle, children throwing
corn to banties. But for now

this clearing above the river
is mine to borrow, burning
the ditch every spring, reviving
country life every season.

Endangered

We watch the river churn gurgles
of autumn enchantment,
the quiet of a country day.

Behind us are the woods,
and we say goodbye
to the iron bridge, awkward now
in its old ways and the journeys
over her rumbling boards
where fishermen tossed down bait
for hopes of catfish.

Today, bats here are protected
because someone hung around nature
long enough to see a food chain.

October will mark
the death of their tree,
dropped like so much kindling,
bereft of lovely limbs
and legions of trembling leaves
to make room
for the new concrete and steel
of bridge construction.

Surrender is never easy,
clinging to past like this tree to sod,
housing this smallest of mammals
with featherless wing.

The Guardsman

Here the sunflowers, there the hummingbird —
equal seekers of sweetness.
— Mary Oliver

He nestles in the thickets with the songbirds,
turning to see the flicker of a tail

like a flickering leaf, the flame of a breast
sweeping against twilight.

He spends days shaping the wilderness,
planting sweet berries to ripen with the seasons,

native trees to draw doves, thrush, finches,
like rose nectar. You must look carefully

to see him among the liatris, the lilies,
the lavender, but he's always there,

always there gathering, weeding, pruning —
the kind caretaker of the gardens.

Turning

and the dreams
tucked like pocket handkerchiefs
into each day
— Naomi Shihab Nye

The clock ticks steady
at the turn of the century,
our ears mindful
of the rhythmic speed.

How easy time marches
to sweep across the cities,
to blow along the countryside.

In Iowa, ditches fill
with wild rose —
fields glisten
with glacial till.

Our minds are fertile
with dreams,
deep and urgent,
that sing to us
with promises to keep.

Iowa Fields

My work is loving the world.
— Mary Oliver

Like an honest face with trusting eyes,
Iowa earth keeps giving.

Isn't it true within all nature
a miracle lives?

To feed the masses is the voice of growth,
the song of prosperity.

Iowa is a fertile land
where homesteads house the caretakers,

where the smile of rain and sun
meets a kernel of corn

like friends who work together.
As long as there is hunger.

The Dance Floor

Sometimes at night
      when air is strangely cool,

I hear her fierce October wind
      lifting paper leaves.

They arabesque, jeté, pirouette,
      going wild in a crazy twirl.

The Leaves at Branson

From my car window
I see October's plush canopy —

maples in fiery crimson,
oaks and elms painted in gold,

the vast, deep green of pine.
I roll down the window

to taste the cold air.
My eyes sparkle with intensity —

how life is most brilliant
before its end

when everything knows
it must let go. Here,

Mother Earth tucks in
her children. Squirrels scamper

beneath anxious hawks
to store nuts for winter.

At New Orleans

Workers at the Dry Dock Company
take their time repairing

an old motor, oil soiling callused
fingers. Sweat stripes their backs

where they winch and strain,
where they work the pumps,

dismantle a boiler.
They listen to slow songs

as a tug puffs down the Mississippi,
ambles for the corner swing,

as the *Cajun Queen* promenades
from the harsh bayous.

Against the current's silver sheen
the *Creole Queen* floats smooth,

effortlessly — three decks
of windows, a smoke stack,

nine flags. The workers
at the Dry Dock Company

play Louie Armstrong's
"That Lucky Old Sun Just Rolls

Around Heaven All Day,"
and the outdoor speaker

moseys Armstrong's voice
across the river's mighty rhythm.

Rainbow;
Edmonton, Canada

until everything
was rainbow, rainbow, rainbow!
— Elizabeth Bishop

One arm spilling into the river,
the other tucked shy

behind a stone building
white with age —

so great is the height of God.
Even her leaving

will be a lesson in beauty,
but for now she stays,

giving us her treasure —
a bridge

over the Saskatchewan
like a masterful painting

that runs through our blood
and deepens blessing

with the brilliance of color
until the blending is simply love.

Traveler

I soar through Seattle's blue vault
to watch the path of the gull
sweep loops against the sky,
coast a stark-white stomach into caps of sea.

I am a pilgrim also loving
my inland home with its warm summers,
the breeze soft against blackberry vines,
bitter winters nipping the air,
junco's quick beaks at the feeder.

I want to slide in among
the thick lanes of Alaskan Way
as if I belong to this place.

Here I sit by a motel window
peering into shimmers of waves
that dance like blinking Christmas lights
beside the Main Fish Company.

The gulls spread their fans,
landing atop the water-beaten pilings.

I step in line to board a ferry,
gliding as though jellyfish
and creatures of the sea are not below,
scurrying from the intrusion.

Is it enough for me to savor Seattle
as a visitor, hearing the rustle of aspen,
this shape of my desire?

Like wind floating amidst bougainvillea
at the end of day, I am a traveler
searching the dying sweetness, letting go.

At the Seattle Pier

The pigeons laugh
when the fisherman
throws the crust,
flinging wheat
over their shoulders.

Like children at play,
they splash puddles
and watch him —
red leggings,
ragged beard.

He stands
to straighten his coat,
drinks from Styrofoam.
It's so simple a thing,
his noontime song.

The Sea's Cathedral

Off the California coast the Garibaldi
damselfish, bright and orange,
gardens his nest meticulously.
Sea lions rock, eat small stones

for ballast. Bat rays float like canopies
over fields of seaweed. The stingray
curls his cape around his shoulders,
and the waves build over the opalescent

squid. Deeper, the swell shark swells up
in a rock crevice, puts her baby
in a *mermaid's purse*. The harbor seal
eats an octopus, retreats in kelp.

Living in a minefield of venom, crab
and jackfish hide in jellyfish. With gills
like a sieve, the angel shark rakes
in plankton. This is the sink of the world.

The Sculpting

*That night we watched you
swimming in the moon.*
— Stanley Kunitz

For a week the Japanese pufferfish
      plows sand into crop circles,

sculpting final touches.
      In the design of a flower six feet

across, it's a stage. When he woos her
      the mate swims over,

unimpressed. He makes
      an alteration. Now the soft sand

is her perfect nest. They dance
      cheek to cheek. Quickly,

he fertilizes her eggs. She swims
      away. He fans the eggs to birth.

Tides

I'm angry at the sea today!
    the small girl in the purple shirt
        tells me on the beach this morning.

        It comes at me and then
    it comes at me again and again
and again! I feel for her —

how the Atlantic rules
    with such vigor, how it never tires.
        Seafoam rushes across my toes.

        A sand crab and sandpiper
    find breakfast. A fisherman
throws out a line. Children shriek,

erect sandcastles. Dogs wag tails.
    I smell the ocean's deepness,
        cower from riptide.

        It's the stunning blue of tides,
    the anguish of a child, waves lifting
again and again and again.

The Loggerhead

the voice
within the voice of the turtle
— Lawrence Ferlinghetti

Luminous as obsidian dragging the shore
    her shell in moonlight across the beach

and behind her the breaking ocean's roar
    to dig her feet in the sandy floor

and lay eggs in the nest her mother bore
    and the fortitude it takes each spring to reach

luminous as obsidian dragging the shore
    her shell in moonlight across the beach.

Waiting for the Pregnant Turtles

Beneath a million brilliant stars,
l stand on the motel's beach approach,
wood and sand beneath my feet,
sea grape brushing an arm.

I wait for the blood moon to rise.
And then it happens —
full, red, magnificent,
the moon swims over the sea.

Is it my imagination,
or do I see illuminated eyes
where pregnant turtles
wade tide's edge, timid and tired,
watching for a safe moment
to climb the beach? I want

to see the loggerheads and greens
or even leatherbacks and flatbacks
when they lumber in the sand
to where they were born, digging
nests with their flippers, laying
their eggs, covering them
with the softness their mothers knew.

But I retreat and grant privacy
to the fortunate few, home at last
where birth is a mother turtle's
finest moment, and babies
are always an astonishment.

Starfish

Tonight, a sea of stars above our heads
as if prolific diamonds spawning stones,
we watch the starfish trail into their beds
like seeds that plant in deeper garden loams.
While spitting tiresome grit from tiny jaws,
their working arms are moving hubs of wheels
until the sinking sand takes final pause —
secure and snug, so soft a nest's appeal.
And now we hear the ocean's rhythm roar
and wonder if the starfish can survive
because we face new waste upon the shore
and feel pollution's danger so alive.
We need an answer to survival's plea —
in the form of cleaning up the sea.

Hurricane

after three days of rain
hearing the wren sing
— W. S. Merwin

Scant moisture off an African coast,
a seed of breeze,
and the next moment
the warm sea gathers

one thunderstorm into another.
You hear of her nightmarish
spinning around a Caribbean eye,
a snake readying her coil to strike,

orphan an island, starve a city.
You watch her path bend close,
life and death a roll of the dice.
She pushes in, spawning tornadoes

beside her. She twists and strips,
floods and steals
every lamp on your nightstand,
every pan in your cupboard,

each drink of water.
If you're fortunate you live,
the throats of your children
again filled with laughter.

Antarctica

When the ice melts along the edges in early afternoon
— Theodore Roethke

At the edge of polar lichen
where sponges grow three feet tall,
sea creatures fill with saltwater
to keep from freezing. No larger
than a watch face, a sea spider grows.

Bull seals broadcast their location —
a thump, thump, thump
like a tire going flat. With large,
sensitive eyes they hunt
the ascending darkness,
every turn a deeper surrender,
starfish and urchins feeding
on their droppings.

In this long night of winter, we could
stop the growth of kidney stones
if we had the antifreeze molecule
of these Antarctic fish.

We wrap in cocoons to study
icebergs two miles thick
where atmospheric ozone can melt
this stretching glacier landscape,
this blue wonder — hidden,
striking, stunningly clean.

The Shape of Rain Clouds

It was the Cretacious period
when all dinosaurs died at once.
Earth shook like a dying star—
a chemical cocktail, a globe
of eruptions. Plunged into drought,
she stained the seas, clouded

the sun. Yet in lonely shallows,
algae shaped into coral.
Bacteria bloomed into larvae,
feeding on sleeping volcanoes.
Magma lifted, piercing Earth's
crust with islands, mountains.

God uncoiled her beautiful wings—
birds dropping seeds across plains
like a flock of angels singing
over the valleys, saving, saving,
saving the world with bright,
flowered faces. We were born,

seeing the shape of rain clouds,
tending wood for the fire.
We populated into the fragrance
of baby toes and cherry pie,
spinning with grandparents'
laughter, dizzy with innovation,
fortified with dreams.

His Return

His Return

Thousands of us celebrate
the Fourth of July, sitting in grasses
surrounded by lilies and Iowa Rose.
Simon Estes sings Old Man River,
and the stagehand releases a flock of doves.
Our necks bend to catch the white flutter
of peace against an overcast sky.

When twilight melts to evening,
I wait for him to call — a trust
as in the fountain near me
with its return and replenish,
return and replenish, tier after tier
of soothing flow. He texts. After
our long wait we exchange messages,
a touch of fingertips, a door opening,
a shift of air.

That which you take to be over
can be a sweet return, like the doves
coming back before flying off again.

Night Rain

I loved how you looked
that first night on my deck,
drawing my chest close to yours
in the rain, the kitchen's half-light
teasing your brown eyes.

So rare are the magical times —
dusk's melt into darkness,
dawn's merge into grey,
as when you kissed me,
and the far-off lights of the horizon
shone like diamonds
in prisms of cut, splendid beauty.

Perhaps the whispered wetness
on our cheeks and shoulders
added to our goose bumps —
that downward climb to our toes
so sudden in its rise again —
almost a blush while we considered
a future of loving,

my beautiful discovery of you
wrapped in each sensual raindrop.

Rose Petals

He says black is my color
when he greets me at the door,
roses in hand.

His face bright as the sun
knowing what roses can do,
he watches my melting.

In his jacket,
handsome and giving,
he reads his eulogy for an uncle,

and somewhere
near the end of each line
his voice softens,

words turning sweet
as apple butter.
He wipes away a tear,

and I busy myself with the roses,
a clip of stem here and there,
small adjustments,

fragrance filling the room.
Each petal is delicate, silken.
Each gift of red, peach,

yellow — exquisite.
My mind in a whirl,
the flowers are safe in water.

Look how he smiles now.
Look how the house paints
a shade of beautiful.

When I Think of You

The stroke of your thumb
against my hand even
when pain is a companion,
your eyes at my very move,
your knowing in times of quiet.

You are the calm tongue
that dissipates darkness,
the ear that hears my faults
and doesn't turn away.

You are ballast, dear,
where things
live and thrive and move,
where things that come apart
settle again.

I need to say this clearly,
absolutely — I love you.

Forgive Me

Homage to William Carlos Williams

I thought of you
when I ate
the glazed raisin
cinnamon rolls,
Caesar salad
with ham, avocado,
and waffle ice cream cones
at the fair.
Forgive me.
It was fabulous.

Hub of Humanity

Despite Guinness at the nearby pub,
Harrod's chocolates

and the falling chill, despite London's
vibrant pulse, a hush falls over

Piccadilly, Soho, Charing Cross
where you and I visit the shops.

Somewhere, somehow,
we are moved by a single stroke

across a violin, almost silent
when it descends touching

our deepest, most reverent thoughts.
Here is the world beside us —

the people of Brazil, Africa, China
in one universal prayer.

The Many Ways

In loving you I bless the many ways.
I love you with the depth a friendship knows
when words can quick go wry with highs and lows
and laughter mends our sudden, clashing frays.
I love you with the gleam in a lover's eyes.
Since I am old my steps have slowed and grace
is a silent poem written on your face
which says that inner beauty never dies.
When I consider moon's bright shine and lift
and how you hold me in your arms so tight,
I think of nearby river's sudden rift,
how countless men have died for what is right,
how rain pours gently down, how quick winds shift,
and love you more with each approaching night.

After the Rain

Sunlight through budding leaves, thunder quieted,
woodpeckers flit from hollows in trees —
sweet stimuli, this giving Earth. I'm thinking
about the neighborhood bobcat stretching
his legs about now, lapping from a puddle
in the timber behind my home. A few of us
have seen him traveling our hills in this spring-
fragranced air, tail bobbing, paws skimming
the grass. With kitten eyes and tufted ears,
he follows the path of deer and turkey before him,
the earth worn from their feet. Past choke cherry
and poison ivy, his searching stride tailed
by hunger, he stops at the creek. He lingers
among reeds, cattails before breaking out again.

And how could I not be thinking of you,
sweetheart, after this rain driving south on I-80,
west on University, the long way to your life-
saving chair? I imagine you unbuttoning your shirt
at the center, the nurse unfastening your port.
Your blood casts off into the tubes, and it's as if
your body is outside your body and becomes
another life as when your father endured dialysis
all those years. The machine is at work
purging the toxins. Fluids empty and fill,
refill and drain. I drive in, wait for you
in the parking lot. You join me, and I wait
for your hands to stop shaking, wait
for your mind to clear before breaking out
for gumbo and sourdough. You and the bobcat,
anything for survival.

TIRED OF GIVING IN

On Slavery

When it is finally ours, this freedom, this liberty, this beautiful
and terrible thing, needful to man as air
— Robert Hayden

The Bantu, a fast runner
and workhorse strong,
is trapped like a lioness,
a profit in the African trade.

Sailing west,
the taskmaster is merciless
as he stands at the bow,
her blood dripping
to the floor of the hold.

In the fields she kisses
bleeding fingers,
the prick of the cotton boll
the same old reminder of pain.

Alone at night in her shack,
a few yellow stars
blinking through slats,
she is a shadow in moonlight.

With ebbing light, she is free.
The pure taste of equality
is sugar on her lips,
the sweet cream of life
finally served.

Harriet Tubman

couldn't read, but she could run.
     It isn't me. It's the Lord!
          she said as she trudged

through Marsh Creek
     again and again, when she
          fended off the copperheads'

close skins across rivers,
     fighting bat wings, owl wings
          at her hair, smelling the dank,

muddy darkness. She followed
     the North Star to Philadelphia
          and safety, hiding slaves

in food pits and basements,
     devising codes and songs
          for the underground.

She was a railroad conductor,
     a suffragette, a scout
          for the Union Army.

Quakers and abolitionists
     called her General,
          but to blacks she was Moses.

Montgomery 1955

White robes like moonlight
In the sweetgum dark.
— Robert Hayden

Rosa was tired of the draft
in the back of the bus, tired
of the cold that clung to her neck
and pressed between her shoulders
like a tumor. It was December 1st,
after all, and even in Alabama
the winter wind swept cruel
into the seats, the surrounding air,
the very oxygen itself. Regardless,
she sat in her designated seat
and fixed her eyes on the ordinary day.

You know the story, how the sign
was moved, how her pupils
blackened in defiance, how
her grip tightened against metal,
how cold the cuffs at her wrists.
She was number 7053. The boycott
lasted over a year. Jim Crow
hadn't yet buried his ugly head.

Rosa was tired of giving in.

Taking a Knee

Martin Luther King
going down at Pettus Bridge,
Colin Kaepernick going down
during the national anthem.

Now a policeman goes down
beside a protester
because George Floyd
and others like him are dead.

Ending racism
is a bridge to be crossed —
a connection to the other side,
a point of moving forward.

Like Jesus when he knelt
at Gethsemane,
where he prayed for himself,
where he prayed for us.

Footsteps

And I hear,
coming over the hills, America singing
— Galway Kinnell

Our Bill of Rights where slavery
remained law, our treacherous past

where Tubman needed to run,
our thirteenth amendment

where blacks still couldn't vote —
it's no surprise that Black Lives Matter

walks the streets of our nation
to see and hear each other

in one humane cause,
when all colors join in footsteps

to civility — when even with
human rights, voting rights,

civil rights, our politicians
still bicker about logic, but isn't it

stunning, how Americans come
together — how we proudly wear

the skin of equality, how humanity
is such a beautiful thing?

Thresholds

From countries broken by anguish,
limping in sorrow, we flee
to America for dreams of hard work
and good rewards. When it is

finally ours to savor — this liberty
essential as breath — we shape
our nests, break open our soil,
remember our war-torn history.

We fathom the trauma of cavalries
chasing buffalo over cliffs,
the shamefulness of white robes
illuminated in firelight. We fight

for our rights and get along in spite
of our differences. We build our nation
brick by brick, mile by mile, through
hope. We create our future with vision

of clarity instead of confusion,
sanity instead of illusion —
and we hold tight our Constitution,
hold high our Bill of Rights.

We the people master our barriers,
create thresholds for others to cross —
because we care, because we dare,
because we're Americans.

Roses

Twenty million women
can't vote. Carrie Chapman Catt
writes to Wilson. He writes back.
They march through Jim Crow,
reconstruction. All races unite.
When World War I explodes,
women join the workforce,
the military. *If we can carry a gun,*
we should vote! Wilson
becomes an advocate.

At the convention
suffragists wear yellow roses,
the vote coming down to Tennessee,
to Henry T. Burn and his red rose.
Burn reads his mother's letter,
Be a good boy and help Mrs. Catt.
The ratification of the Nineteenth
Amendment to the United States
Constitution passes.

Burn became a yellow rose.

Bouquets of Jellied Gasoline

A red-winged blackbird,
buffy rim like a colonel's wing bar,
sits on a lone branch of the jungle
searching for grubs in the swamp.

Smoky blue napalm thick in humid air,
a bath of blood covering your fatigues,
you watch the apocalypse,

listen to the blackbird's call:
conk-err-ee--check,
conk-err-ee--check,

say goodbye to Joe Freestone,
the Mekong River a tomb,
Joe's epitaph a ripple.

You have lunch with the President,
show him the gape of your wound,
bitter, unhealed.

And slip quiet into another world.

Guernica

Death has a life of its own
in Picasso's pose of despair.

Everything is involved —
men, bulls, horses,

jagged, severed, taken.
Even today in kitchens

where neighbors sip coffee,
the craze of war remains alive.

Bones broken like bodies
of the Spanish Civil War,

entire cities
are green on canvas.

Driven sleepless,
Picasso painted the mother

holding her dead child —
each stroke a warning,

each crazy eye open
and watching.

In the Deep Night of Winter

In spite of terror,
in spite

of the soldier's accurate aim in the dark —
a starlight scope

mounted on his missile-launcher —
I am searching for sounds

of the season:
the quiet of snowdrops

asleep in their bulbs
waiting to wake in a sudden thaw,

murmurs of peace
in the deep night of winter,

murmurs that the snowshoe hare
hiding from the snowy owl

will soon be eaten.
The sound of tomorrow cries

bold, brave in spruce and pine,
even the wind unflinching.

INFINITY

We Believed in Angels

the eye like the eye of faith believes.
— Robert Hayden

We sat like three parishioners in a pew,
discussing angels, the ones we knew,

and Paul's road to Damascus.
Books across laps,

test scores on our minds;
we believed in angels.

Through the glass wall,
sun met fluorescent bulbs, technology.

She, a nurse — he, a teacher —
more stories told. We counted them,

neglecting the new ones at our side,
wearing glasses, studying.

In the Beginning

there is fire. First
light, first universe, birth
in a genesis — blue, red,
yellow plasma born
exquisite in space.

Imagine how a speck
in this energy expands, how
the big bang transforms
a wave, a particle, a proton
into matter.

Here, first stars
radiate heat. Here,
first galaxies, this
cosmic revolution, gather
in stunning diversity.

Here, the green sun
and planets and moons,
individual as juggling balls,
precede hydrogen.
And Earth. Here is life,

the beginning of us.
Then, the unimaginable.
Da Vinci's oil and tempera
on dry wall says it best —
the Son of God. Infinity.

You Included Me

when you died on the cross,
nailed as a criminal.

For a Jew to be crucified
was the highest form of mocking.

For you to withdraw your life
that I should live

shatters within my mind.

At Calvary

Hung as deer skin stretching
to dry in hot afternoon sun,
the lamb is ready for sacrifice.
His feet nailed to the saddle,

soldiers offer wine and gall
to tease his thirst,
cast lots for clothing.
They laugh at his limp body

where the steel sword
impales his side, where
nails goad palms fast to wood.
The black close of darkness

surrounds the days until
he rises brighter than sun,
yoking every man's blood
to the disaster.

Communion

all things born with wings
that sing
— Lawrence Ferlinghetti

Dust of snow mute
upon the shag of hickory,

wind silent
where it sweeps Earth's mantle,

how tender his breath,
how calm his feet

on the path
where before a storm was raging.

The sound of forgiveness
is hushed —

a finger pressed to lips,
a holy, quiet tongue.

Listen to the Children

Had I the heavens' embroidered cloths,
Enwrought with golden and silver light
— Yeats

Let the children come.
Hear their innocence.
See teachings of giving

in pudgy fingers and eyes
clear with trust. Untouched
by thought of darkness

they dance with rain beating
on flawless skin.
They do not question the rain,

apples within easy reach,
ceilings above silken heads.
They know this springtime

will be spread across land, sky,
universe, the heavens,
and all beyond.

About the Author

Pat Underwood grew up on an Iowa farm across the horizon from where she and her husband raised their two sons. She retired in 2017 from her work in early education and working for the State of Iowa. Since her husband's death, she remains on their country hillside near Colfax, IA surrounded by poetry-inspiring nature. Her publications include three poetry books: *Where I Live* (Blue Light Press 2022), *Portraits* (Finishing Line Press 2017), and *Gatherings* (Celestial Light Press 2007). Her play kit *The Last Supper* (Meriwether Publishing Ltd.; Contemporary Drama Service 1997) travels the nation. Underwood's poems received a 2001 Pushcart Prize Nomination, a 1996 Founder's Award, and a 2002 Founder's Award from the National Federation of State Poetry Societies. Recently, she was chosen as the winner of the 2025 Vinnie Ream Letters Contest sponsored by the National League of American Pen Women.